Home-Tested
Slow Cooker
Recipes
14 slow cooker recipes from real people like you!

bbq beef sandwiches

1 boneless beef chuck roast (about 3 pounds)
¼ cup ketchup
2 tablespoons brown sugar
2 tablespoons red wine vinegar
1 tablespoon Dijon mustard
1 tablespoon Worcestershire sauce
1 clove garlic, crushed
¼ teaspoon salt
¼ teaspoon liquid smoke
⅛ teaspoon black pepper
10 to 12 French rolls or sandwich buns

1. Place beef in slow cooker. Combine remaining ingredients except rolls in medium bowl; pour over meat in slow cooker.

2. Cover and cook on LOW 8 to 9 hours.

3. Remove beef from slow cooker; shred with 2 forks. Combine beef with 1 cup sauce from slow cooker. Evenly distribute meat and sauce mixture among warmed rolls.

Makes 10 to 12 servings

Susan says: This recipe keeps beautifully in the fridge once it is cooked. Just reheat it in the microwave or on your stove top.

Favorite recipe from ***Susan Revely, Ashland, KY***

bbq beef sandwich

cheesy slow cooker chicken

6 boneless skinless chicken breasts (about 1½ pounds)
Salt
Black pepper
Garlic powder
2 cans (10¾ ounces each) condensed cream of chicken soup, undiluted
1 can (10¾ ounces) condensed Cheddar cheese soup, undiluted
Chopped fresh parsley (optional)

1. Place 3 chicken breasts in slow cooker. Sprinkle with salt, pepper and garlic powder. Repeat with remaining 3 breasts and seasonings.

2. Combine soups in medium bowl; pour over chicken. Cover; cook on LOW 6 to 8 hours or until chicken is no longer pink in center. Garnish with parsley before serving, if desired.

Makes 6 servings

Joan says: The sauce is wonderful over noodles, rice or mashed potatoes.

Favorite recipe from ***Joan VandenNoven, Beloit, WI***

honey ribs

1 can (10¾ ounces) condensed beef consommé, undiluted
½ cup water
3 tablespoons soy sauce
2 tablespoons honey
2 tablespoons maple syrup
2 tablespoons barbecue sauce
½ teaspoon dry mustard
2 pounds pork baby back ribs, trimmed

1. Combine consommé, water, soy sauce, honey, maple syrup, barbecue sauce and mustard in slow cooker; mix well.

2. Cut ribs into 3- to 4-rib portions. Add ribs to slow cooker. (If ribs are especially fatty, broil 10 minutes before adding to slow cooker.)

3. Cover; cook on LOW 6 to 8 hours or on HIGH 4 to 6 hours or until ribs are tender. Cut into individual ribs. Serve with sauce.

Makes 4 servings

Donna says: These ribs are delicious alone, but are even better served with rice.

Favorite recipe from ***Donna Urbanek, Levittown, PA***

chinese cashew chicken

- **1 pound fresh bean sprouts *or* 1 can (16 ounces) bean sprouts, drained**
- **2 cups sliced cooked chicken**
- **1 can (10¾ ounces) condensed cream of mushroom soup, undiluted**
- **1 cup sliced celery**
- **½ cup chopped green onions**
- **1 can (4 ounces) sliced mushrooms, drained**
- **3 tablespoons butter**
- **1 tablespoon soy sauce**
- **1 cup whole cashews**
- **Hot cooked rice**

1. Combine bean sprouts, chicken, soup, celery, onion, mushrooms, butter and soy sauce in slow cooker; mix well.

2. Cover; cook on LOW 4 to 6 hours or on HIGH 3 to 4 hours.

3. Stir in cashews just before serving. Serve with rice.

Makes 4 servings

Barb says: Serve with rice or noodles.

Favorite recipe from ***Barb Gartzke, Sullivan, WI***

slow cooker stuffed peppers

1 package (about 7 ounces) Spanish rice mix
1 pound ground beef
½ cup diced celery
1 small onion, chopped
1 egg, beaten
4 medium green bell peppers, halved lengthwise, cored and seeded
1 can (28 ounces) whole peeled tomatoes, undrained
1 can (10¾ ounces) condensed tomato soup, undiluted
1 cup water

1. Set aside seasoning packet from rice. Combine beef, rice mix, celery, onion and egg in large bowl. Divide meat mixture evenly among pepper halves.

2. Pour tomatoes with juice into slow cooker. Arrange filled pepper halves on top of tomatoes. Combine tomato soup, water and reserved rice mix seasoning packet in medium bowl. Pour over peppers. Cover; cook on LOW 8 to 10 hours. *Makes 4 servings*

Favorite recipe from ***Susan Ambrose, Cabot, PA***

chili with beans and corn

- 1 can (15 ounces) black-eyed peas or cannellini beans, rinsed and drained
- 1 can (15 ounces) kidney or navy beans, rinsed and drained
- 1 can (14½ ounces) whole tomatoes, drained and chopped
- 1 onion, chopped
- 1 cup frozen corn
- 1 cup water
- ½ cup chopped green onions
- ½ cup tomato paste
- ¼ cup diced jalapeño peppers*
- 1 tablespoon chili powder
- 1 teaspoon ground cumin
- 1 teaspoon prepared mustard
- ½ teaspoon dried oregano leaves

**Jalapeño peppers can sting and irritate the skin. Wear rubber gloves when handling peppers and do not touch your eyes. Wash hands after handling.*

Combine all ingredients in slow cooker. Cover and cook on LOW 8 to 10 hours or on HIGH 4 to 5 hours. *Makes 6 to 8 servings*

swiss steak

1 onion, sliced into thick rings
1 clove garlic, minced
1 beef round steak (about 2 pounds), cut into 8 pieces
All-purpose flour
Salt
Black pepper
1 can (28 ounces) whole tomatoes, undrained
1 can (10¾ ounces) condensed tomato soup, undrained
3 medium unpeeled potatoes, diced
1 package (16 ounces) frozen peas and carrots
1 cup sliced celery

1. Place onion and garlic in slow cooker.

2. Dredge steak in flour seasoned with salt and pepper. Shake off excess flour. Place steak in slow cooker. Add tomatoes with juice. Cover with tomato soup. Add potatoes, peas and carrots and celery.

3. Cover; cook on LOW 6 to 8 hours or until meat and potatoes are tender. *Makes 8 servings*

Amy says: I sometimes add corn or green beans. This recipe is very easy and definitely a family favorite!

Favorite recipe from ***Amy Rivera, Arlington, VA***

italian combo subs

1 tablespoon vegetable oil
1 pound boneless beef round steak, cut into thin strips
1 pound bulk Italian sausage
1 green bell pepper, cut into strips
1 medium onion, thinly sliced
1 can (4 ounces) sliced mushrooms, drained (optional)
Salt
Black pepper
1 jar (26 ounces) pasta sauce
2 loaves French bread, cut into 6-inch pieces and split

1. Heat oil in large skillet over medium-high heat. Brown beef strips in two batches. Place beef in slow cooker.

2. Brown sausage in same skillet, stirring to separate meat. Drain and discard fat. Add sausage to slow cooker.

3. Place bell pepper, onion and mushrooms, if desired, over meat in slow cooker. Season with salt and black pepper. Top with pasta sauce. Cover; cook on LOW 4 to 6 hours. Serve in bread rolls.

Makes 6 servings

Serving Suggestion: Top with freshly grated Parmesan cheese.

Favorite recipe from ***Valorie Rowland, Hardin, KY***

italian combo sub

red beans and rice with ham

1 package (16 ounces) dried red beans
1 pound beef smoked sausage, sliced
1 ham slice (about 8 ounces), cubed
1 small onion, diced
2½ to 3 cups water
1 teaspoon Mexican (adobo) seasoning with pepper
⅛ teaspoon ground red pepper

1. Soak beans overnight; rinse and drain.

2. Place beans in slow cooker. Add sausage, ham, onion and water (2½ cups for LOW or 3 cups for HIGH). Season with Mexican seasoning and red pepper.

3. Cover; cook on LOW 7 to 8 hours or on HIGH 3 to 4 hours or until beans are tender, stirring every 2 hours, if necessary. Serve over rice.

Makes 6 servings

Cheryl says: Serve over white rice.

Favorite recipe from ***Cheryl Hulbert, Newnan, GA***

clam chowder

- **5 cans (10¾ ounces each) condensed reduced-fat cream of potato soup, undiluted**
- **2 cans (12 ounces each) evaporated skimmed milk**
- **2 cans (10 ounces each) whole baby clams, rinsed and drained**
- **1 can (14¾ ounces) cream-style corn**
- **2 cans (4 ounces each) tiny shrimp, rinsed and drained**
- **¾ cup crisp-cooked and crumbled bacon (about ½ pound) or imitation bacon bits**
- **Lemon pepper to taste**
- **Oyster crackers**

Combine all ingredients except crackers in slow cooker. Cover; cook on LOW 3 to 4 hours, stirring occasionally. Serve with oyster crackers. *Makes 10 servings*

Favorite recipe from ***Karen Bassett, Citrus Heights, CA***

chicken and stuffing

- **½ cup all-purpose flour**
- **¾ teaspoon seasoned salt**
- **¾ teaspoon black pepper**
- **4 to 6 boneless skinless chicken breasts (about 1 to 1½ pounds)**
- **¼ cup (½ stick) butter**
- **2 cans (10¾ ounces each) condensed cream of mushroom soup, undiluted**
- **1 package (12 ounces) seasoned stuffing mix, plus ingredients to prepare mix**

1. Combine flour, seasoned salt and pepper in large resealable plastic food storage bag. Add chicken; shake to coat with flour mixture.

2. Melt butter in large skillet over medium-low heat. Brown chicken on both sides. Place in slow cooker; pour soup over chicken.

3. Prepare stuffing according to package directions, decreasing liquid by half. Arrange stuffing over chicken. Cover; cook on HIGH 3 to 4 hours. *Makes 4 to 6 servings*

Favorite recipe from ***Anna Ertl, Franksville, WI***

cantonese pork

- **2 pork tenderloins (about 2 pounds)**
- **1 tablespoon vegetable oil**
- **1 can (8 ounces) pineapple chunks in juice, undrained**
- **1 can (8 ounces) tomato sauce**
- **2 cans (4 ounces each) sliced mushrooms, drained**
- **1 medium onion, thinly sliced**
- **3 tablespoons brown sugar**
- **2 tablespoons Worcestershire sauce**
- **1½ teaspoons salt**
- **1½ teaspoons white vinegar**
- **Hot cooked rice**

1. Cut tenderloins in half lengthwise, then crosswise into ¼-inch-thick slices. Heat oil in large nonstick skillet over medium-low heat. Brown pork on all sides. Drain and discard fat.

2. Place pork, pineapple with juice, tomato sauce, mushrooms, onion, brown sugar, Worcestershire, salt and vinegar in slow cooker.

3. Cover; cook on HIGH 4 hours or on LOW 6 to 8 hours. Serve over rice.

Makes 8 servings

Favorite recipe from ***Stacy Pineault, Mahwah, NJ***

easy beef stroganoff

- **3 cans (10¾ ounces each) condensed cream of chicken or cream of mushroom soup, undiluted**
- **1 cup sour cream**
- **½ cup water**
- **1 package (1 ounce) dry onion soup mix**
- **2 pounds beef for stew**

Combine soup, sour cream, water and dry soup mix in slow cooker. Add beef; stir until well coated. Cover; cook on on LOW 6 hours or on HIGH 3 hours. *Makes 4 to 6 servings*

Mary says: Serve this beef over hot cooked wild rice or noodles along with a salad and hot bread. You can reduce the calories and fat in this dish by using 98% fat-free soup and nonfat sour cream.

*Favorite recipe from **Mary Braam, Raleigh, NC***

best ever slow cooker pot roast

1 beef chuck shoulder roast (3 to 4 pounds)
1 can (10 ounces) beef gravy
1 package (1 ounce) au jus gravy mix
½ package Italian salad dressing mix
½ cup dry red wine
2 tablespoons all-purpose flour
½ cup cold water

1. Place roast in slow cooker. Combine gravy, au jus mix, salad dressing mix and wine in medium bowl. Pour mixture over meat. Cover; cook on LOW 8 to 10 hours.

2. Remove roast to plate; cover with foil to keep warm. Turn slow cooker to HIGH. Mix flour into water until smooth. Stir into juices in slow cooker. Cook 15 minutes or until thickened. Serve gravy with roast. *Makes 8 servings*

Favorite recipe from ***Ann Foster, Redlands, CA***